♥

A Mum's love for her child is unconditional, even in the animal kingdom.

We all need our Mums to protect, nurture and look after us.

Baby animals love their Mums and learn from them every day, just like us.

♥

I'm so glad I look like you Mum, because your face is beautiful.

Koalas are marsupials, which means a mother keeps her baby in a special pouch. When a koala baby is too big for the pouch, it clings onto its mother's back while she clambers through eucalyptus trees.

I love
Mum

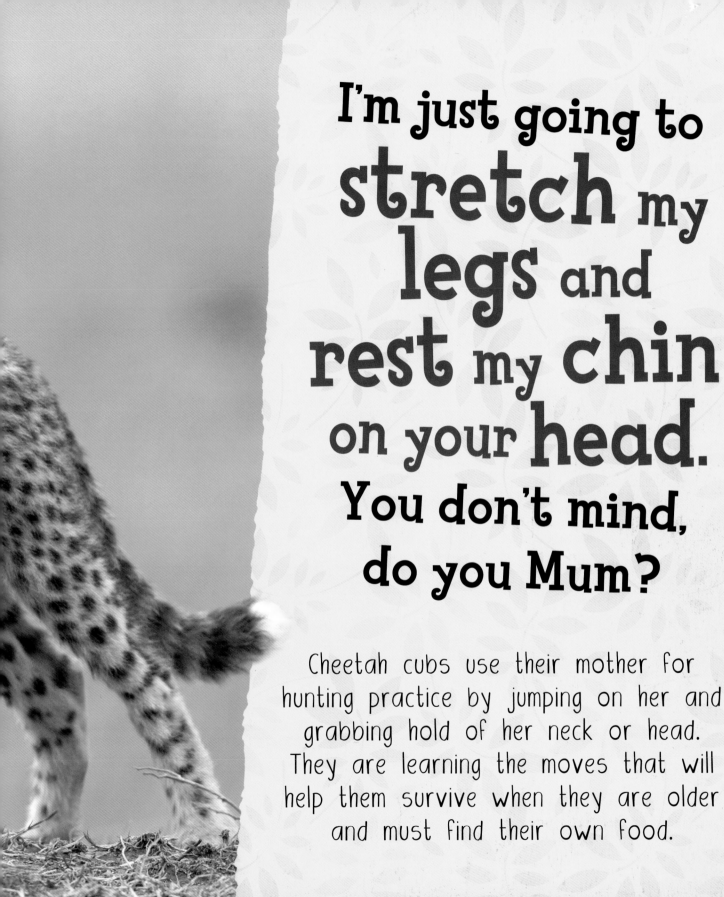

I'm just going to **stretch** my **legs** and **rest** my **chin** on your **head.** You don't mind, do you Mum?

Cheetah cubs use their mother for hunting practice by jumping on her and grabbing hold of her neck or head. They are learning the moves that will help them survive when they are older and must find their own food.

Oh no, it's gone all dark. Where is everyone?

Piping plovers are great parents.
They let their chicks huddle underneath
them to keep warm. They even
pretend to be injured so other
animals attack them, not their babies.

Your smile lights up my world.

A dolphin calf can swim as soon as it is born. It gets an easy ride by staying next to its mother. As she moves through the water the calf is pulled along, too. Dolphins 'talk' to each other with clicks and whistles.

I know you want the best for me, Mum. Wherever you lead, I will follow.

Mother elephants and their babies have a very close, loving bond. Female calves often stay with their mothers all their lives and grandmothers help raise the next generation of youngsters.

We're playing hide and seek. Don't tell Mum where I'm hiding!

A baby kangaroo is called a joey. The joey climbs into its mother's pouch as soon as it has been born, and is no bigger than a jelly bean. A pouch is a safe place to drink Mum's milk and grow bigger.

Sometimes the world looks big and scary, but I feel safe when I'm close to my Mum.

The world is a scary place for a gazelle because lions and hyenas are on the lookout for animals to hunt. Mothers force their newborn babies onto their feet so they will be ready to run if there is any sign of danger.

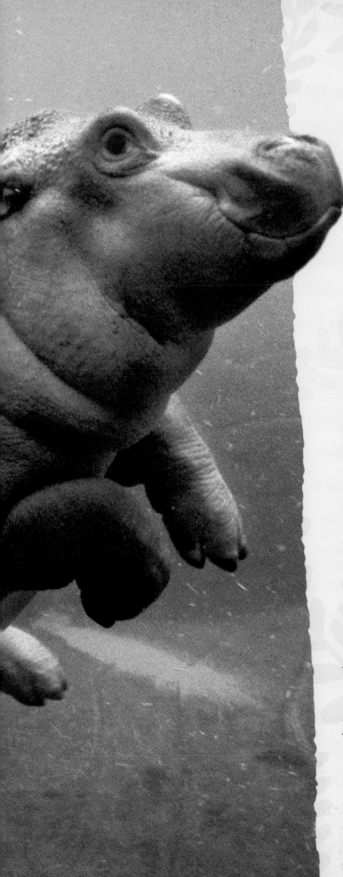

My Mum's always there for me, even when I need a little nudge...

Hippos are huge, heavy animals that spend most of the day wallowing in cool water. They have massive teeth – up to 51 centimetres long – and can deliver a deadly bite to anyone who comes too close to their calves.

You always offer me a shoulder to cry on when I'm feeling sad.

Lemurs only live on the island of Madagascar. Most lemur mothers carry their babies everywhere they go until they are at least four months old. They feed them, clean them and teach them how to find food.

LOOK at me, Mum! LOOK at what I can do!

Baby orang-utans cling to their mothers until they are about two years old, but they are learning from her all the time. They like to grab hold of branches and practise swinging or gripping with their fingerlike toes – but they always keep Mum close by!

I promise
to have a bath, Mum...
right after you have had yours.

Grey wolves live in family groups called packs. Only the top male and female in a pack have cubs, but all the wolves work together to protect the family and hunt for food. Cubs are born blind, deaf and helpless.

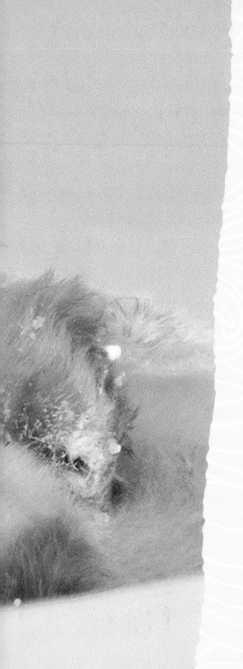

I love you SO much. I just want to cuddle with you forever!

Polar bears live in one of the world's coldest places. They have incredibly thick fur so they can cope with icy wind and they can even swim in chilly Arctic waters. Their white colour helps to camouflage them in the snow.

My Mum supports me in everything I do. She is my rock.

Mother walruses are huge, but male walruses grow twice as big – up to 4 metres long! Walrus pups climb onto their mother's back so they can watch the world from a safe place without getting squashed by clumsy males!

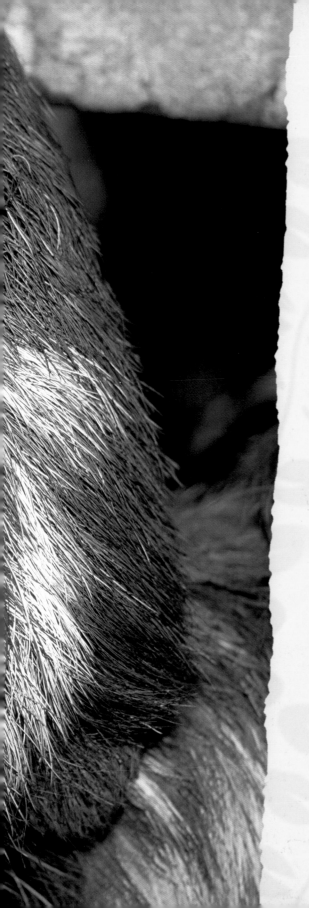

Mum says it's time for bed. Sweet dreams!

Sloths live in rainforest trees. They move so slowly that plants can grow in their fur, giving it a greenish tinge. They sleep while hanging upside-down and only clamber down to the ground once a week, when it is time to poo!

Here are three ways to show Mum you love her.

Give her a big hug.

♥

Draw her a beautiful picture.

♥

Ask her about her day.

Can you think of any more?

Editor: Tasha Percy
Designer: Natalie Godwin
Publisher: Zeta Jones

Copyright © QED Publishing 2014

First published in the UK in 2014 by
QED Publishing
A Quarto Group company
The Old Brewery, 6 Blundell Street,
London, N7 9BH

www.qed-publishing.co.uk

A catalogue record for this book is available from the British Library.

ISBN 978 1 78493 143 8

Printed in China

Photo credits
(t=top, b=bottom, l=left, r=right, c=center, fc=front cover)
1c: naturepl.com: Eric Baccega, 2c: Foto Natura: Flip De Nooyer, 3r: Shutterstock:
Background, 4l: Shutterstock: Background, 5r: naturepl.com:Tony Heald, 6c: Frans
Lanting Stock: Frans Lanting, 7r: istockphoto.com: Background, 8l: Shutterstock:
Background, 9r: naturepl.com:Anup Shah, 10c: FLPA: ImageBroker, 11r: istockphoto.
com: Background, 12l: Shutterstock: Background, 13c: FLPA: Suzi Eszterhas, 14c: FLPA:
Christian Hütter,15r: Shutterstock: Background, 16l: istockphoto.com: Background,17r:
Getty Images; (c) Paul Souders, 18c: Minden Pictures:Tim Fitzharris, 19r: Shutterstock:
Background, 20l: Shutterstock: Background, 21c: Minden Pictures: Suzi Eszterhas, 22c:
Foto Natura: Stephen Belcher, 23r: Shutterstock: Background, 24l: istockphoto.com:
Background, 25r: Corbis: © Frans Lanting, 26l: FLPA: Suzi Eszterhas, 27r: Shutterstock:
Background, 28l: Shutterstock: Background, 29r: FLPA: Mitsuaki Iwago, 30l: ZSSD, 31r:
Shutterstock: Background, 32c: Shutterstock: Background, tl:
© Biosphoto: Michel & Christine